Read the Signs

Abby Jackson
Illustrated by Sheila Bailey

Rigby®

A Harcourt Achieve Imprint

www.Rigby.com
1-800-531-5015

One beautiful day, Fox and Mouse
took a walk.
They were going down the path
when . . . *Swish!*
A big, gold leaf fell on Mouse's head.

"That is a sign," Fox said.

"What kind of sign?" asked Mouse.

"You will know soon enough," said Fox.
"Let's keep walking."

Fox and Mouse saw Owl.
Owl came outside to say hello.
They were talking when . . . *BRRR!*
A cold wind blew Owl's feathers.

"That is a sign," said Fox.

"What kind of sign?" asked Owl.

"You will know soon enough," said Fox.
"Let's keep walking."

Fox, Mouse, and Owl saw Rabbit
sitting in the green grass.
Rabbit hopped up to join them
when . . . *Zip!*
A pumpkin rolled right over
Rabbit's foot.

"That is a sign," said Fox.

"What kind of sign?" asked Rabbit.

"You will know soon enough," said Fox.
"Let's keep walking."

Fox, Mouse, Owl, and Rabbit
saw Squirrel in his tree.
Squirrel's cheeks were full.
Squirrel tried to speak
when . . . **MMMMPH!**
A nut popped out of Squirrel's mouth.

"That is a sign," said Fox.

"What kind of sign?" asked Squirrel.

"You will know soon enough," said Fox.
"Let's keep walking."

Fox, Mouse, Owl, Rabbit, and Squirrel saw their friend Bear.

Bear said, "The days are getting shorter. I am getting very sleepy."

"That is a sign," said Fox.

"What kind of sign?" asked Bear.

"You will know soon enough," said Fox.
"Let's keep walking."

Fox, Mouse, Owl, Rabbit, Squirrel, and
Bear saw Goose swimming in the pond.

Goose said, "I have to go south now.
I will join my friends down there."

"That is a sign," said Fox.

"What kind of sign?" asked the animals.

"You will know soon enough," said Fox.
"Let's keep walking."

The friends went up a big hill.
They went around a tree.
They saw many animals and
a lot of food.

The animals shared the food.
Some animals ate enough
to last them all winter.
Other animals gathered food
to take home.
Then they all said goodbye.

"Now you know," said Fox.
"Now you know how to read the signs
that say . . . fall is here!"